My First Animal Kingdom Encyclopedias

FISH

by Lisa J. Amstutz

Consultant:
Jackie Gai, DVM
Wildlife Veterinarian

CAPSTONE PRESS
a capstone imprint

A+ Books are published by Capstone Press,
1710 Roe Crest Drive, North Mankato, Minnesota 56003
www.mycapstone.com

Library of Congress Cataloging-in-Publication data is available on the Library of Congress website.
ISBN 978-1-5157-3929-6 (library binding)
ISBN 978-1-5157-3940-1 (paperback)
ISBN 978-1-5157-3969-2 (eBook PDF)

Summary: A photo-illustrated reference guide to fish that highlights physical features, diet, life cycles, and more.

Editorial Credits

Kathryn Clay, editor; Rick Korab and Juliette Peters, designers;
Kelly Garvin, media researcher; Gene Bentdahl, production specialist

Photo Credits

Getty Images/Fairfax Media, 30 (tr); Minden Pictures: Florian Graner, 23 (t), Hiroya Minakuchi, 30 (br), Jelger Herder/Buiten-beeld, 23 (m), (b), Norbert Wu, 21 (b), 31 (br); Shutterstock: abcphotosystem, 11 (m), Adam Ke, 29 (bm), Andrea Izzotti, 8, 25 (tm), 28 (tm), (b), Andrey_Kuzmin, 10-11 (bkg), 24-25 (bkg), apathosaurus, 18 (bl), Aries Sutanto, cover (tl), Beth Swanson, 19 (tr), Catmando, 20 (b), 22 (t), cbpix, 5 (t), Daniel Huebner, 18 (br), David Litman, 28 (tl), Dmitrijs Mhejevs, 30 (bl), Dmitriy Komarov, 10 (r), Dmytro Pylypenko, 13 (bm), Dray van Beeck, 24 (t), Erni, 28 (tr), Evgheni Manciu, 1 (l), Ingrid Prats, 32, J. Bicking, 15 (b), Jeffrey M. Frank, 14 (b), Jill Lang, 25 (b), Johnny Adolphson, 27 (b), Jonpaul Hosking, 12 (b), Kalenik Hanna, 30-31 (bkg), Kangcor, 16-17, kaschibo, 30 (tl), keren-seg, 4-5 (bkg), 12-13 (bkg), 22-23 (bkg), khwanchai, 13 (t), Kim David, 29 (tm), Kristina Vackova, 19 (tl), 21 (tm), 31 (tr), Krzysztof Odziomek, 25 (t), Kyle Lippenberger, 4 (b), LauraD, 11 (tl), Leonardo Gonzalez, cover (br), 9 (inset), lolloj, 29 (tr), LorraineHudgins, 22 (b), Mark Caunt, 15 (m), Matt9122, 6-7, Melinda Fawver, 15 (t), Nantawat Chotsuwan, 1 (r), Nicram Sabod, 29 (tl), nitrogenic.com, 9, nudiblue, 13 (b), Patryk Kosmider, cover (bl), Piotr Krzeslak, 5 (b), rangizzz, 14-15 (bkg), 20-21 (bkg), 28-29 (bkg), Rada Photos, 28 (bm), Rich Carey, 11 (tr), (b), 27 (tr), (tl), 31, (tl), Richard Williamson, 18-19 (bkg), Ronnie Chua, 14 (t), Sergey Lavrentev, 21 (t), Sergey Uryadnikov, 10 (l), SeraphP, 18 (t), 21 (bm), Shane Gross, 20 (t), Sphinx Wang, back cover, Stasis Photo, 26 (b), Studio 37, 8 (inset), Suphatthra China, 5 (m), Tatyana Vyv, cover (tr), Thomas Hasenberger, 20 (m), twospeeds, 31 (bl), Ugo Montaldo, 26 (t), Vadim Petrakov, 12 (t), Vagabonddivan, 25 (bm), Videologia, 13 (tm), wildestanimal, 24 (b), Willyam Bradberry, cover (bkg), 1 (bkg), 26-27 (bkg), Yann Hubert, 19 (b), 29 (b)

Artistic elements: Shutterstock: Kalenik Hanna, Miceking, pinare

Printed in the United States of America.
10025S17

TABLE OF CONTENTS

What Are Fish?

Fish are animals that live only in water. There are about 28,000 kinds of fish. Some are smaller than a fingernail. Others are larger than a school bus!

class
a smaller group of living things; fish are grouped into three classes

phylum
(FIE-lum)
a group of living things with a similar body plan; fish belong to the phylum Chordata (kawr-DEY-tuh); mammals, amphibians, birds, and reptiles are also in this group

kingdom
one of five very large groups into which all living things are placed; the two main kingdoms are plants and animals; fish belong to the animal kingdom

order
a group of
living things that
is smaller than a
class; there are
62 orders
of fish

cold-blooded
also called ectothermic
(EK-tuh-THER-mik);
cold-blooded animals have
a body temperature that is
the same as the water
or air around them;
nearly all fish are
cold-blooded

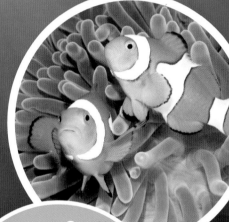

vertebrate
(VUR-tuh-brit)
an animal that has
a backbone; fish
are vertebrates

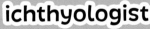

species
(SPEE-sees)
a group of animals
that are alike and
can produce young
with each other

ichthyologist
(ik-thee-OL-uh-gist)
a scientist who
studies fish

Super Swimmers

Fish are made for swimming. Their slippery bodies slide easily through water.

float
to move slowly through water or air without sinking

swim bladder
a sac filled with air inside the body of a fish; swim bladders help fish float

tail
the part at the back end of a fish's body that pushes it through water

streamlined
designed to move easily and quickly
through air or water; most fish have
smooth, narrow, streamlined bodies

slime
a slippery mixture that
covers the bodies of some
fish; slime helps protect
fish from disease

scales
small, hard plates that
cover the skin of most fish

gill
a body part used to breathe
underwater; all fish have gills

fin
a body part that fish use
to swim and steer in water

From Egg to Adult

Fish hatch from eggs. Some female fish lay their eggs in water. Others carry them inside their bodies. Young fish grow fast. Soon they will have young of their own.

life cycle
the series of changes that take place in a living thing, from birth to death

fry
young fish

live young
babies born directly from their mother, rather than from eggs; guppies carry their eggs inside their bodies and then give birth to live young

spawn
to lay eggs in water

roe
a mass of fish eggs

life span
the number of years a certain animal usually lives; small bettas have a life span of up to three years, while some koi can live more than 100 years

growth rings
rings on the scales of a fish; scientists can count these rings to learn the age of a fish

adult
a fully grown animal

juvenile
(JOO-vuh-nahyl) a young animal that is not fully grown

school
a large number of the same kind of fish swimming and feeding together

What's for Dinner?

Finding food is a full-time job for fish. Some feed on plants. Some eat other animals. Some eat both!

carnivore
(KAHR-nuh-vor): an animal that eats only meat; most sharks are carnivores

predator
(PRED-uh-tur): an animal that hunts other animals for food; the piranha is a predator

prey
(PRAY): an animal hunted by another animal for food; small fish are prey for larger fish and other animals

food chain
a series of living things in which each one eats the one before it

herbivore
(HUR-buh-vor): an animal that eats only plants; parrotfish eat algae growing on coral reefs

omnivore
(OM-nuh-vor): an animal that eats both meat and plants; the queen angelfish is an omnivore

scavenger
(SKAV-in-jer): an animal that feeds on animals that are already dead; hagfish are scavengers

hunt
to chase and kill animals for food

algae
(AL-jee): small plants without roots or stems that grow in water

seaweed
a plant that grows underwater

In Salty Seas

Salt water tastes terrible—unless you're a fish! Many kinds of fish live in salt water. They make their homes in salty oceans and seas all around the world.

ocean
a large body of salt water; many fish live in the oceans

sea
an area of salt water that is part of an ocean; seas are partly enclosed by land

salt water
water that is salty; salt water is found in oceans

marine
(muh-REEN): living in salt water

habitat
the type of place and conditions in which a plant or animal lives

range
the larger area where an animal mostly lives

estuary

(ES-choo-air-ee): the area where a river meets the sea; water in an estuary is slightly salty

plankton

tiny plants and animals that drift in water; many fish feed on plankton

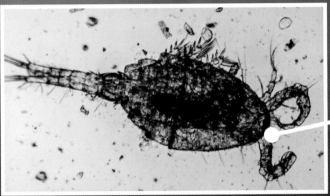

krill

a small, shrimplike animal; salmon feed on krill in the ocean

polar

having to do with the icy areas around the North or South Pole; polar fish usually live near the ocean floor

reef

an underwater strip of rocks, coral, or sand near the surface of the ocean

Keeping It Fresh

Many fish live in freshwater
habitats, such as rivers and lakes.
Some stay there year-round.
Others swim from rivers to the sea.

freshwater
water that does not contain salt;
most ponds, rivers, lakes, and
streams are freshwater bodies

dam
a wall that stretches across a
river; dams slow down rushing
water and raise the water level
behind them; dams can block
traveling fish

fish ladder
a series of steps that allows fish
to swim over a dam or waterfall

downstream
the direction the water
in a stream flows

upstream
against the flow of water
in a stream

brackish
a mix of salt water
and freshwater

hatchery
a place where people allow
fish to hatch from eggs

fish farm
a place where fish are raised
for food; tilapia are often
farmed in lakes

migrate
(MYE-grate): to move from
one place to another when
seasons change in order to
find food or to mate

leap
to jump over something;
salmon leap up waterfalls
and fish ladders

run
to move up or down a river
to spawn; striped bass run
up rivers to spawn and then
return to the ocean

Sensing the World

Fish have the same five senses that you do—plus a few more! Staying alert helps them stay alive.

electric current
a flow of energy made by some fish; they use the electricity to protect themselves or to stun their prey

pit organs
body parts that may help fish find prey by sensing electric currents; scientists are not exactly sure what these organs do

taste buds
groups of cells that sense flavors; some fish have taste buds on their fins, mouths, and tails

barbel
a whisker-like feeler on the head of some sharks and other fish; fish use barbels to taste

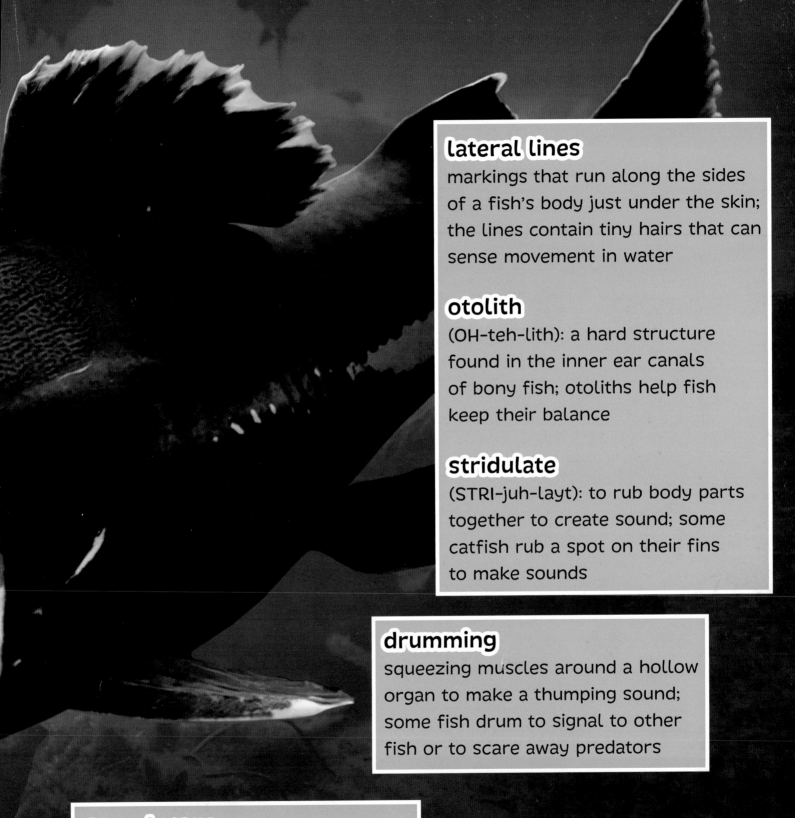

lateral lines
markings that run along the sides of a fish's body just under the skin; the lines contain tiny hairs that can sense movement in water

otolith
(OH-teh-lith): a hard structure found in the inner ear canals of bony fish; otoliths help fish keep their balance

stridulate
(STRI-juh-layt): to rub body parts together to create sound; some catfish rub a spot on their fins to make sounds

drumming
squeezing muscles around a hollow organ to make a thumping sound; some fish drum to signal to other fish or to scare away predators

sound wave
a movement or vibration that can be heard; sound waves travel easily through water

17

Staying Safe

It's a dangerous world out there. A hungry predator may be hiding behind the next rock. How can a little fish stay safe?

spine
a sharp, pointed growth; the lionfish's venomous spines keep predators away

warning coloration
bright markings on some fish that warn predators to stay away; some fish with warning colors are poisonous

poisonous
(POI-suh-nuhs) containing a harmful substance that causes sickness or death when touched and/or eaten

jump
flying fish can jump into the air to escape danger

hide
to keep out of sight; some fish hide from predators

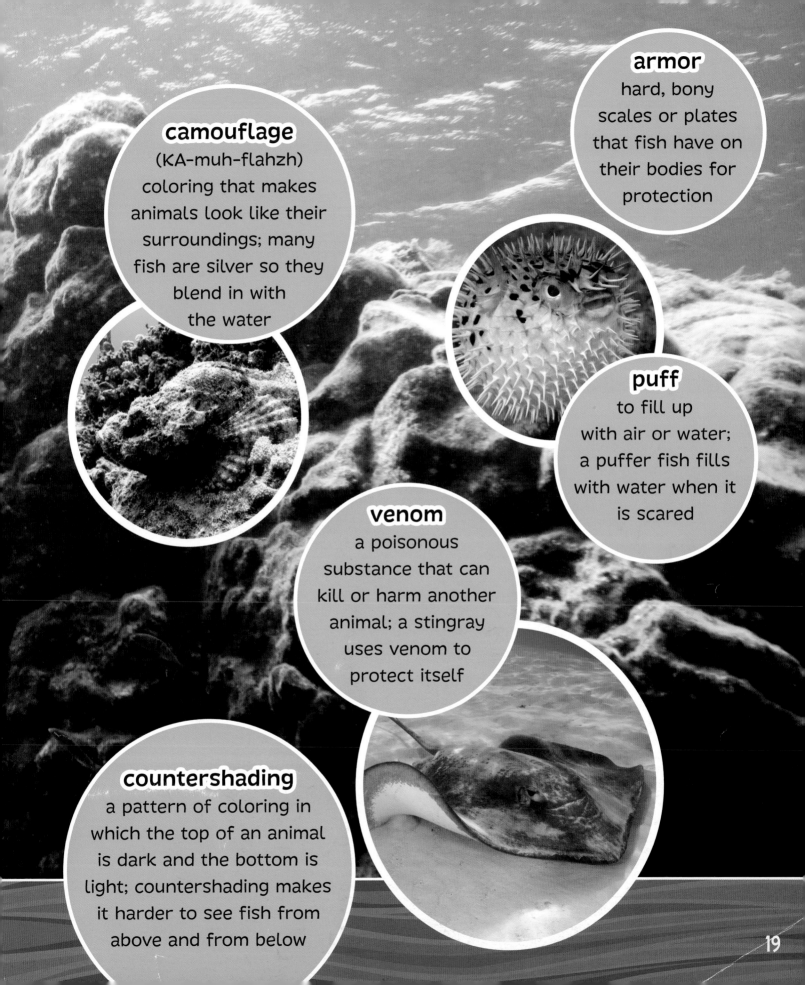

camouflage
(KA-muh-flahzh)
coloring that makes
animals look like their
surroundings; many
fish are silver so they
blend in with
the water

armor
hard, bony
scales or plates
that fish have on
their bodies for
protection

puff
to fill up
with air or water;
a puffer fish fills
with water when it
is scared

venom
a poisonous
substance that can
kill or harm another
animal; a stingray
uses venom to
protect itself

countershading
a pattern of coloring in
which the top of an animal
is dark and the bottom is
light; countershading makes
it harder to see fish from
above and from below

Bony Fish

Fish fall into three main groups called classes. The largest group is the bony fish. These fish have jaws and a bony skeleton.

skeleton
the bones that support and protect the body of an animal

tuna
a large, silvery fish often caught for food

sturgeon
a large freshwater fish; humans often catch sturgeon for food

scute
(SKOOT): a flat, bony growth on some fish; the sturgeon has five rows of thick scutes instead of scales

coelacanth
(SEE-luh-kanth): an ancient fish that is still found in oceans today

gar
a freshwater fish covered with hard, diamond-shaped scales; gar have long jaws with needlelike teeth

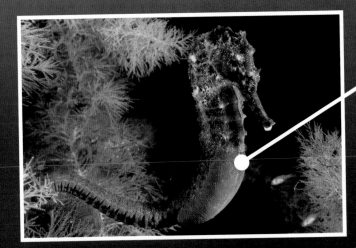

flounder
a flat fish with eyes on top of its head

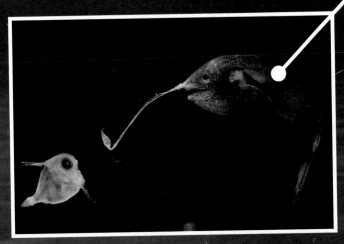

sea horse
a bony fish that swims upright; its head is shaped like a horse's head

anglerfish
female anglerfish have a special spine that sticks out; they use it to attract nearby prey

Fish Without Jaws

The most ancient group of fish
is the jawless fish. Only two types
of jawless fish are still
alive—hagfishes and lampreys.
The others are extinct.

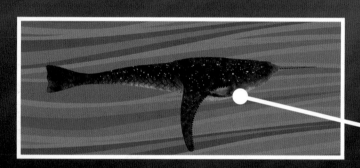

jawless
having no jaws; hagfishes and
lampreys are jawless fish

Agnatha
(AG-nuh-thuh): the class
of jawless fish

extinct
(ek-STINGKT): no longer
living; an extinct animal is
one that has died out, with
no more of its kind on Earth;
Doryaspis nathorsti is an
extinct jawless fish

fossil
(FAH-suhl): the remains
or traces of living things
preserved as rock; many
jawless fish are found
as fossils

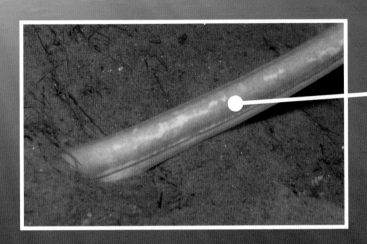

hagfish
an eel-shaped fish; hagfish hide in burrows on the ocean floor until they smell a dead animal

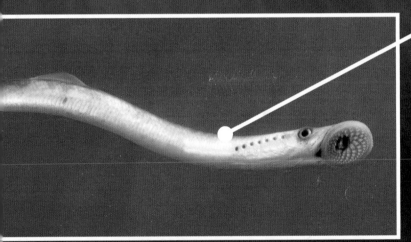

lamprey
a fish that can live in freshwater or salt water; lampreys latch onto other fish and feed on their blood

parasite
an animal or plant that lives on or inside another animal or plant; lampreys are parasites

tooth plate
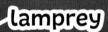
teeth that are joined together to form sharp, horny plates; lampreys use their tooth plates to bite through the scales and skin of their prey

Squishy Fish

The last group of fish is the cartilaginous fish. Fish in this group have jaws. But they don't have hard bones. They have softer cartilage. Rays, skates, and sharks belong in this group.

dorsal fin
a fin located on the back of a fish; sharks are known for their large dorsal fins

gill slits
body parts in the sides of some fish through which they breathe; most sharks have five to seven gill slits on each side of their bodies

cartilage
(CAR-tuh-lij): the strong, bendable material that forms some body parts on animals

pectoral fin
(PEK-ter-ul fin): one of two fins found where the head meets the body

spiracles
tiny holes through which some animals breathe; rays and skates have spiracles behind their eyes

wing
one of two wide, flat pectoral fins that skates and rays use to swim

snout
the long front part of an animal's head; many sharks have long snouts

mermaid's purse
the hard egg case of a skate

pup
a young shark

sawfish
a type of ray with a long, saw-shaped snout

A Dangerous World

Fish face many dangers. Humans cause some of these dangers. We must all work together to keep water clean and safe for fish.

endangered
in danger of dying out; the Southern bluefin tuna is one of the world's most endangered fish

climate change
changes in weather patterns caused by human activities

pollution
materials that harm the air, water, and soil

overfishing
to take so many fish from an area that the species is in danger of dying out

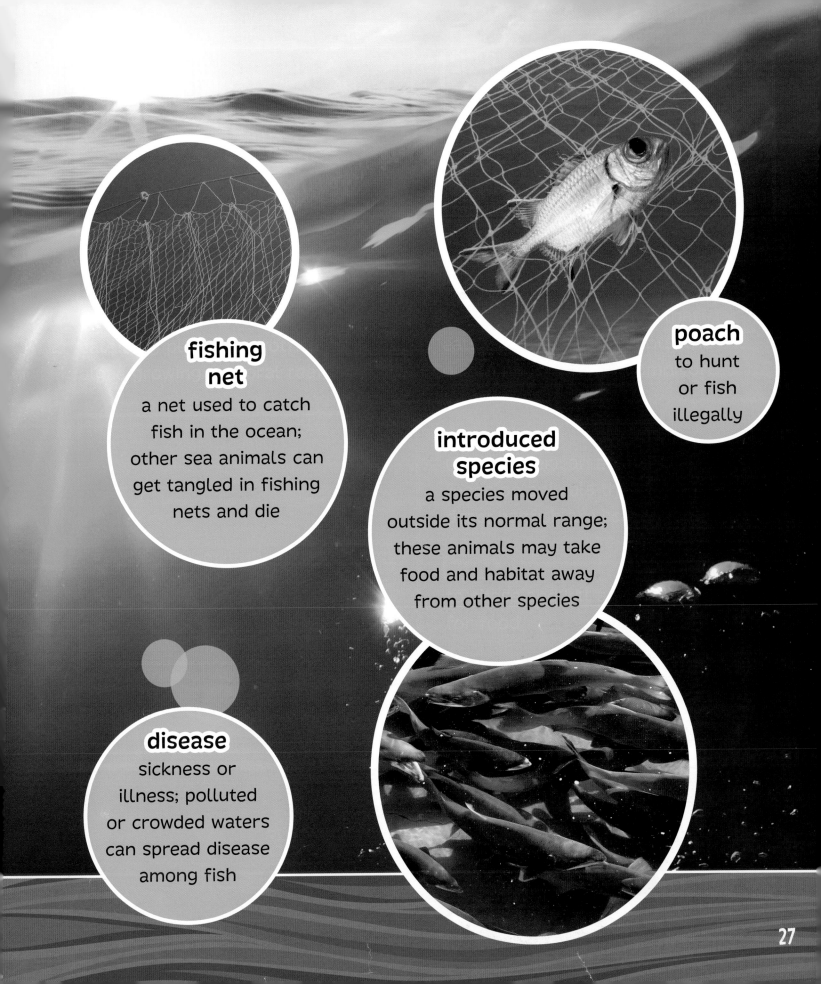

fishing net

a net used to catch fish in the ocean; other sea animals can get tangled in fishing nets and die

poach

to hunt or fish illegally

introduced species

a species moved outside its normal range; these animals may take food and habitat away from other species

disease

sickness or illness; polluted or crowded waters can spread disease among fish

Sounds Fishy!

Their names may sound fishy. Their bodies may look fishy. But these animals are not really fish!

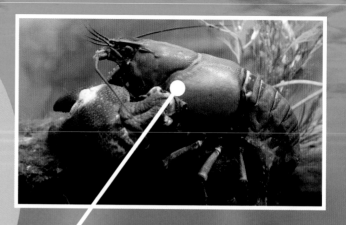

crayfish
a hard-shelled animal with two large pincers; crayfish are crustaceans

cuttlefish
a mollusk with eight arms

dolphin
a fish-like mammal that lives in the ocean; dolphins are warm-blooded and feed milk to their young

jellyfish
a sea animal with a soft, almost clear body and tentacles

manatee
a large, plant-eating mammal with two flippers and a wide, spoon-shaped tail

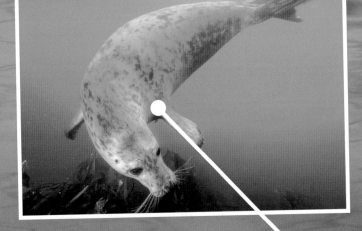

salamander

an amphibian that may live in or out of the water; most salamanders have four legs

seal

a sea mammal that has fur and flippers and lives in coastal waters

shellfish

an animal with a hard shell; clams, oysters, and crabs are shellfish

starfish

a marine animal shaped like a star, with five or more arms

whale

a large mammal that lives in the ocean; whales come to the surface to breathe air

Fun Facts

The **whale shark** is the largest fish. It can reach 40 feet (12 meters) or more in length.

You have to look closely to see a **stout infantfish**. The female of this species is only 0.25 inches (6.4 millimeters) long.

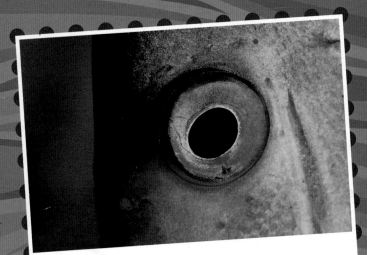

Fish have **no eyelids**. They sleep with their eyes open.

A cheetah would have trouble keeping up with a **sailfish**. This fish can swim up to 70 miles (113 kilometers) per hour.

A **moray eel** has two sets of jaws—one in its mouth and one in its throat.

People in Japan eat the deadly **puffer fish**. Chefs must have special training to prepare it.

Some fish can "walk" on land. The **mudskipper** uses its fins as legs.

The **flashlight fish** gives off a greenish glow to attract its prey. The glow comes from bacteria in pockets under its eyes.

READ MORE

Goldsworthy, Kaite. *Fish.* Life Cycles. New York: AV2 by Weigl, 2014.

Lewis, Clare. *Fish Body Parts.* Animal Body Parts. Chicago: Heinemann-Raintree, 2016.

Royston, Angela. *Fish.* Animal Classifications. Chicago: Heinemann-Raintree, 2015.

INTERNET SITES

FactHound offers a safe, fun way to find Internet sites related to this book. All of the sites on FactHound have been researched by our staff.

Here's all you do:
Visit *www.facthound.com*
Type in this code:
9781515739296

Super-cool stuff!

Check out projects, games and lots more at **www.capstonekids.com**